MARCELINE'S
World of Vampireness

by Kirsten Mayer

PSS!
PRICE STERN SLOAN
An Imprint of Penguin Group (USA) LLC

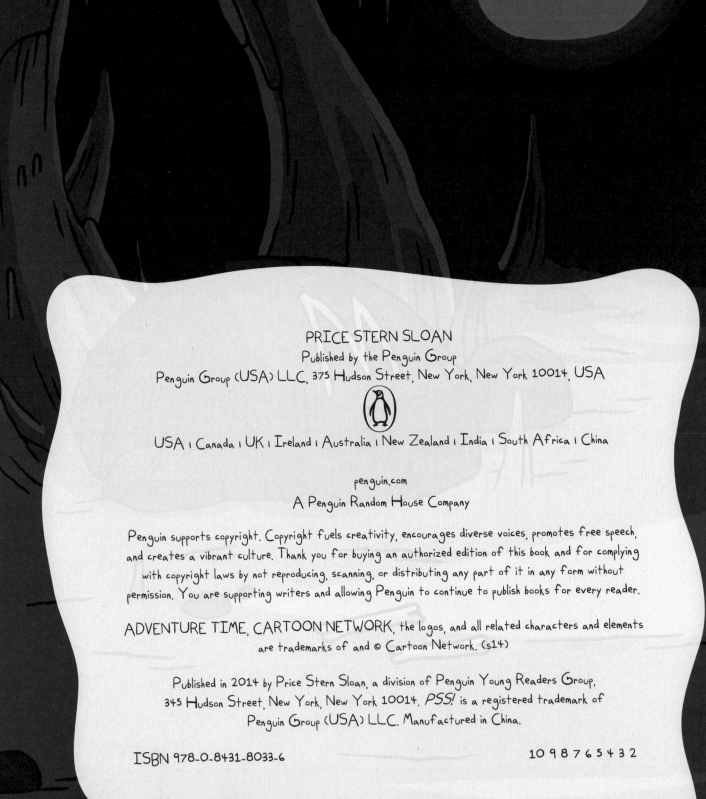

PRICE STERN SLOAN
Published by the Penguin Group
Penguin Group (USA) LLC, 375 Hudson Street, New York, New York 10014, USA

USA | Canada | UK | Ireland | Australia | New Zealand | India | South Africa | China

penguin.com
A Penguin Random House Company

Published in 2014 by Price Stern Sloan, a division of Penguin Young Readers Group, 345 Hudson Street, New York, New York 10014. PSS! is a registered trademark of Penguin Group (USA) LLC. Manufactured in China.

ISBN 978-0-8431-8033-6   10 9 8 7 6 5 4 3 2

CHILLIN' CROSSWORD

Answer all these questions about Marceline and then fill in the words either across or down. Do it now, or Marceline will turn you into a ghost!

DOWN
1. What did Marceline's father eat that upset her?
2. Marceline's _____ rules the Nightosphere
3. What is Hambo?
9. What is Marceline's ex-boyfriend's name?

ACROSS
4. What can't Marceline see in her mirror?
5. What does Marceline wear when she's ruling the Nightosphere?
6. What color does Marceline like to eat?
7. Marceline claims she rode giant _____ in the ocean on her travels
8. What sport do Marceline, Jake, and Finn play outside of her house?
10. What treasured item did Marceline give Princess Bubblegum?

AX ME SOMETHING

Circle all the instruments that Marceline has played.

BORED TO ROCK

Now draw a more radical instrument for her to jam on!

WHAT'S YOURS IS MINE

Use the stickers to help Marceline reclaim the Tree Fort she had waaaay before Finn and Jake did.

So you think you're smart, huh, henchman? Prove it.

TRY THIS.

2	5	4	3		1		6	
	1		4		6	5	2	3
6	9			8		1	7	4
1		7		8	9	2		
9	8	5	6			7		
3		2	1	4		8		5
5	7		9		8		1	2
8	3	9	2	1	4	6	5	
4	2	1		6	5	3		9

Oh yeah? How about this one?

		5	9			7	2	6
	3				5		7	1
8	6	7		4	1		5	
6		1	4			8	9	
		3			6	5	4	7
		4	3				1	
1			5	2		7	3	6
7		2	1	6				
	4			7				5

You think you are *sooo* clever. Well . . .

2	9	7		8			4	
				9				8
		4	2	3		1		
				7		2	5	
	3	2		1				
6	7	5		2				1
5		3	9		2			
	1					3		2
				6	3	9		

I'm over a thousand years old, and
I can't do this one. I dare you.

4						8	2	
7				3				
	9			4		1		
		4		6		3		1
3		7					8	
				9			7	
6	2		7			5	9	
		9				4		
1			3					

FIGHT TO WRITE

Marceline's a bodacious bass player with a veracious voice. Come up with some lyrics for a new song for her.

WHAT'S THE DIFF?

Henchman, tell me the differences between these two pictures. And after that, go strangle some pixies.

WORD UP!

Find these words in the puzzle. They can appear up, down, across, or diagonal.

```
M U S H R O O M W A R R H U X
S N U U I J D V W J Y A A R S
Q U H F I R E K I N G D O M E
H U N S O N A B A D E E R R D
T T E L U M A K Q V U W E T F
Y C T G I R P B E M Z H B T E
G H L M Z G A C N E P V A V L
V A T A T S H N E S V B T N E
D M F R S T N T O Z E O G V L
E B D C F W W T H P D D A W O
M O M E P T H O L T K M C O J
O L E L M G A X N P P F L L N
N W Z I I G J V A I T B Z F A
L J R N D S E W R O C Q R Z B
V U C E X E D E G V G F Z B M
```

HAMBO

NIGHTOSPHERE

VAMPIRE

DEMON

SUNLIGHT

BAT

BASS

BANJOLELE

AMULET

MARCELINE

FIRE KINGDOM

HUNSON ABADEER

MUSHROOM WAR

WOLF

LOST AND FOUND

After living for over a thousand years, Marceline has kind of lost her moral code. Help her through the maze so she can find it again. Or whatever.

START

FINISH!

MEMORIZE WITH YOUR EYES

Marceline has seen some things that would make you say, *Like what?* Take a long look at her adventures on these pages, then turn the page and see how much you can remember.

1. What color is the fish that Marceline is riding?
....

2. What is Marceline doing in the Fire Kingdom?
....

3. Where does the creature spray its ink?
....

4. How many fish are there in total?
....

5. How many nut creatures is she holding?
....

6. What colors are they after they've been crushed?
....

7. Which hand is she holding them in?
....

8. What color is her Hula-Hoop?
....

9. What do all the nut creatures have on them?
....

10. What is Marceline wearing on her feet?
....

CODE RED

You've made it this far, henchman, but I want to give you another test. I need to make sure you are smart enough, and I need to see how well you really know me. Crack the code below, or else.

= A   = B   = C   = D   = E

= F   = G   = H   = I   = J

= k   = L   = M   = N   = O

= P   = Q   = R   = S   = T

= U   = V   = W

= X   = Y   = Z

"

"

" ___ _____ ___ ___ ___

___ ___ ___ ___ ___

___ ___ ___ ___ ___ !"

21

Marceline has been alive for over one thousand years. That's a long freakin' time, dude! What are some of the things she did in her first four hundred years? Write some ideas down here.

Was born

Played a kazoo

Tied her shoes

Went to her first rock concert

Was bitten by a vampire

PIN THE LIMBS ON THE HAMBO

Use your stickers to pin the limbs on the Hambo! Oh, and to give him back his button eye, too.

RHYME TIME

List words that rhyme with "Marceline the Vampire Queen."

FINISH MARCELINE'S JOURNAL ENTRY

Or just jam some stickers here . . . whatever floats your goat.

Dear Journal,

Hello, Journal, it's me.
It's been a while since we've talked about my life and stuff.

Marcie's Secret Feelings

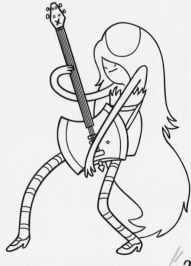

DUNK IN

Marceline, Finn, and Jake like to play hoops. Marceline can even dunk without floating! Use your apple and fork-and-spoon stickers to challenge a friend to a fair game of tic-tac-toe.

SNACK TIME

Marceline eats only one color. Circle all the stuff she could eat on this page.

29

BAD DAD

Which of these Hunson Abadeers is the real one? Look for the one that's different from the others.

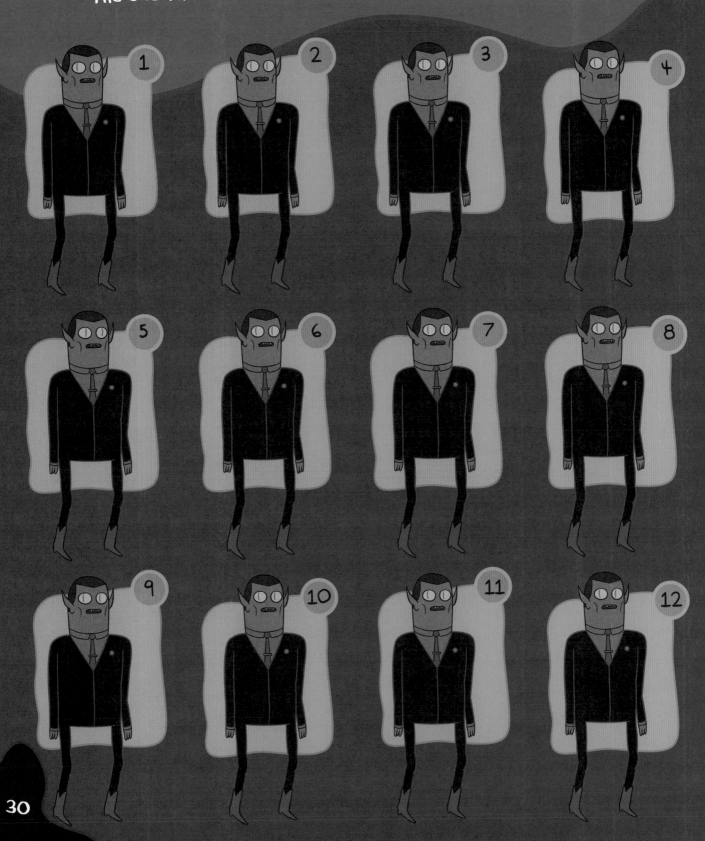

WILL YOU BE MY FRIEND?

BMO had a system error. Help BMO unscramble these words!

KAANPESC _____

CROCES _____

AGASUSE _____

BONTUT _____

TERRCLOONL _____

YESTRYM _____

HOSHRUBOTT _____

ABRASKETOD _____

LOFTOBAL _____

BRAYETT _____

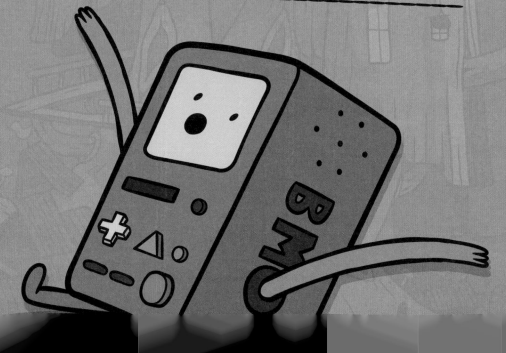

HAND VERSUS HAND

Like Finn, Marceline is ambidextrous, meaning she can dunk a basketball with either hand. See if you have the same talent. Try drawing the same picture with your left hand and then with your right hand. For an extra challenge, try drawing with both hands at the same time!

HOW TO DRAW MARCELINE

Follow these step-by-step instructions and draw a pic of Marceline!

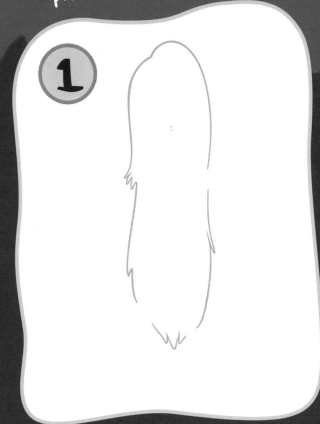

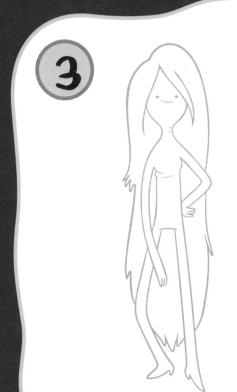

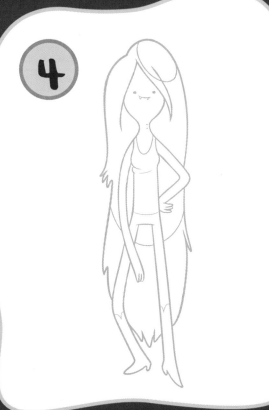

UNDEAD PET PARADE

The Vampire Queen's pet zombie poodle is named Schwabl. If you had a zombie pet, what would it be? Draw it here. Give it a name!

ADVENTURE TIME
BINGO BONGO

Next time you watch the boob tube and catch some eps of *Adventure Time*, pay attention for once! When you hear one of the words or see one of the characters on the game board, cover that space with a coin or a button. When you fill a whole row, shout out BINGO BONGO! Congrats, you won a game against yourself.

A NIGHT IN THE NIGHTOSPHERE

Grab a die and use your stickers or some random doodads as game pieces. Finn and Jake dare you to have an adventure as epic as theirs—try it with this Nightosphere board game!

You're in a jail cell full of bananas. **LOSE ONE TURN!**

← **GET IN LINE!** You have to go 28 spaces before you can see the Teller.

SEE THE TELLER. Just kidding! You have to wait in another line. Roll again.

There's a storm cloud killing demons! You hide behind a rock and lose a turn.

THE CASTLE

PORTAL TO HOME

CONGRATS!

YOU WIN!

ARMY OF SKELETONS

Marceline can raise the dead. How many skeletons did she get on their feet? Count as many as you can on this page.

WHO'S THAT EX?

Connect the dots to see which ex-boyfriend Marceline axed.

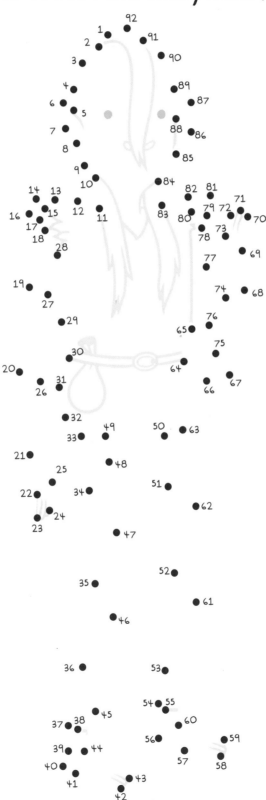

Marceline has been alive for over one thousand years. That's a long freakin' time, dude! What are some of the things she did during years 401 to 800? Write some ideas down here.

Fought an ogre

Met some ghosts

Turned into a wolf. Turned back.

Ate something red

HIDING IN PLAIN NIGHT

How many amulets can you find hidden in the Nightosphere?

HOW TO DRAW HAMBO

Steps below. Follow them. Draw a Hambo . . . you know the drill.

①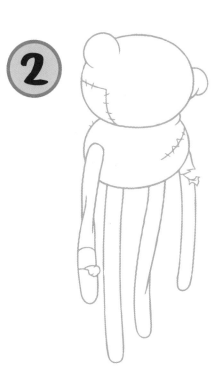

②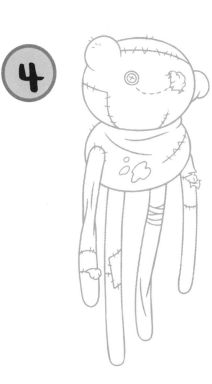

③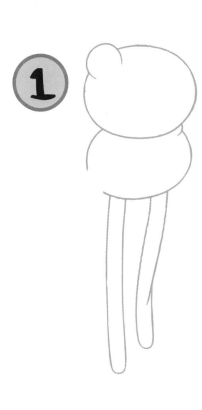

④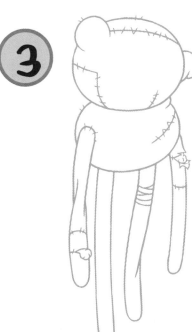

ADVENTURE STORY TIME

Here are some scenes from one of Marceline's most epic pranks. In the spaces below the images, write in what happened, or make up a new story to go with them!

PIECES of ME

Marceline wrote some song lyrics and then hated them, so she ripped up the paper. Can you put the pieces back together and see what she wrote? Write the lyrics down below.

I hope
And like
want you
don't wan

you under
the way tha
respe   and
to   the N

rule

stand
I am
I wanna be her
Nightosphere.

'Cause I
But I

50

FLY BY WOLF

Marceline can levitate—and she flies through the forest chasing a pack of wolves. Help her find the right path to their wolf den.

START→

FINISH

FIRE FINDER

Finn and Jake come home to find that Marceline has lit candles throughout their home as a prank. Find them all so Finn and Jake can blow them out!

SHIFTY BUSINESS

You might have seen Marceline in a form that wasn't quite . . . human. The Vampire Queen can change shapes! Circle all the forms she can take on below.

NIGHT SHIFT

If you were a half-vampire, half-demon chick, what shape would you want to take? Draw it here.

HANG TIME

Marceline and Princess Bubblegum are hanging out for the day . . . what should they do? Draw some rad ideas here.

T-BONES

PB loves the rock-band shirt Marceline gave her a long time ago. It's pretty awesome. Design some of your own rock-band shirts here.

SLICE of LIFE, PART 3

Marceline has been alive for over one thousand years. That's a long freakin' time, dude! What are some of the things she did in the last two hundred years? Write some ideas down here.

Met a cool dude named Finn

Lived in a tree house

Played the bass

Snuggled with Schwabl

ANSWERS

Pages 4–5

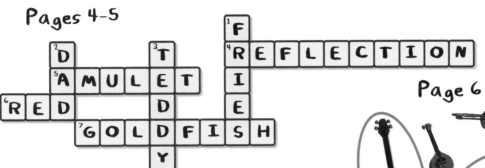

The crossword answers:
- 1. FRIEND (down, F-R-I-E-N-D)
- 2. DAMULET / AMULET
- 3. TEDDYBEAR (down)
- 4. REFLECTION
- 5. AMULET
- 6. RED
- 7. GOLDFISH
- 8. BASKETBALL
- 9. ALLSTASH / SPLASH (down)
- 10. TSHIRT

Page 6

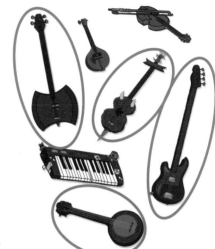

Pages 10–11

TRY THIS.

2	5	4	3	7	1	9	6	8
7	1	8	4	9	6	5	2	3
6	9	3	8	5	2	1	7	4
1	4	7	5	8	9	2	3	6
9	8	5	6	2	3	7	4	1
3	6	2	1	4	7	8	9	5
5	7	6	9	3	8	4	1	2
8	3	9	2	1	4	6	5	7
4	2	1	7	6	5	3	8	9

You think you are sooo clever. Well . . .

2	9	7	6	8	1	5	4	3
3	5	1	7	9	4	2	6	8
8	6	4	2	3	5	1	9	7
1	8	9	3	4	7	6	2	5
4	3	2	5	1	6	7	8	9
6	7	5	8	2	9	4	3	1
5	4	3	9	7	2	8	1	6
9	1	6	4	5	8	3	7	2
7	2	8	1	6	3	9	5	4

Oh yeah? How about this one?

4	1	5	9	3	7	2	6	8
2	3	9	6	8	5	4	7	1
8	6	7	2	4	1	3	5	9
6	7	1	4	5	2	8	9	3
9	2	3	8	1	6	5	4	7
5	8	4	3	7	9	6	1	2
1	9	8	5	2	4	7	3	6
7	5	2	1	6	3	9	8	4
3	4	6	7	9	8	1	2	5

I'm over a thousand years old, and I can't do this one. I dare you.

4	3	1	9	7	6	8	2	5
7	5	8	1	3	2	9	4	6
2	9	6	5	4	8	1	3	7
9	8	4	2	6	7	3	5	1
3	6	7	4	5	1	2	8	9
5	1	2	8	9	3	6	7	4
6	2	3	7	1	4	5	9	8
8	7	9	6	2	5	4	1	3
1	4	5	3	8	9	7	6	2

Pages 14-15

Page 16

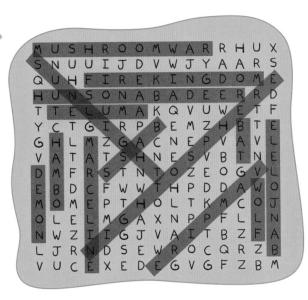

Page 17

Page 20
1. Orange
2. Hula-Hooping
3. Finn's face
4. Two
5. Five
6. Red, green, yellow, blue, and pink
7. Her right hand
8. Green
9. Stars
10. Cowboy boots

Page 21
"A radical dame who likes to play games!"

Page 29

Page 40
There are 42 SKELETONS
in the picture.

Page 30

Page 41

Page 31

PANCAKES
SOCCER
SAUSAGE
BUTTON
CONTROLLER
MYSTERY
TOOTHBRUSH
SKATEBOARD
FOOTBALL
BATTERY

It's Ash!

Pages 44–45
There are eighteen amulets hidden in the picture.

Page 50

Page 51

Page 54

Pages 52–53

YOUNG MARCELINE

SIMON PETRIKOV

HUNSON ABADEER

FINN

JAKE

FRIES

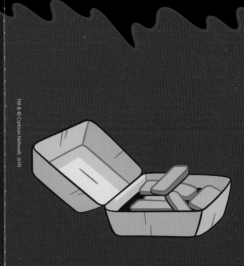

MARCELINE

MARCELINE MONSTER FORM

MARCELINE BAT